FREE YOUR MIND

What we think about has a direct effect on our feelings and actions. Win over anxiety, negativity, and depression, and free your mind.

Daniel Boyd

Unless otherwise noted, all scripture quotes are taken from the *New International Version,* Copyright © 1973, 1978, 1984, 2011 by Biblica, Inc.

Copyright © 2024 Daniel Boyd
All rights reserved.
ISBN: 9798327694491

Dedication

To Billie, my love, my wife, and my partner in life and ministry. For nearly five decades God has used you to help me be a better Christ follower, husband, father, and pastor, in that order. I love you!

Table of Contents

Dedication……………………………………………..…..iii

Introduction…………………………………………..…..vi

Chapter One - Paying Attention………………..1

Chapter Two - Thought Bombs…………………7

Chapter Three - Weapons for Battle………..21

Chapter Four – Next Weapon…………………..31

Chapter Five – So, Fight!……..…..……………..41

Chapter Six – The Normal Mind………………..53

Chapter Seven – Overcoming Depression..71

Chapter Eight – Overcome………………………..89

Bibliography…………………………………..…………109

Introduction

Our actions are a direct result of our thoughts. What we choose to think about has a direct connection to how we act and feel. In this book, I hope you will learn how to be selective about what you let into your mind and how to free your mind from damaging unrighteous negative thoughts.

What's more, as a Christ follower, we have an invisible enemy who can and does throw his "flaming arrows" at us to attack our mind with unrighteous and condemning thoughts. We must defend ourselves against these flaming arrows with the shield of faith, as we read in Ephesians 6. We need to know the word of God well enough to align the thoughts that we are having with the word of God. And so, there is a struggle that goes on in our minds. Who will win this fight?

Sensory overload. There is so much information available to us now and so many images coming our way via the screens that we view that our brain is often overloaded and on occasion wants to shut down. We find ourselves scrolling on our tablet or smart phone, swiping every few seconds. Before we know it, we have "zoned out" and cannot remember a thing. I believe this has contributed to our very short attention spans and inability to focus for extended periods of time.

2 Corinthians 10:4–5 says that we are to rid ourselves of any thought that exalts itself above the word of God. I think of it like this: When an ungodly thought comes into my mind and as it were, I grab hold of it and instantly compare it to scripture. If it does not line up, I cast it out and turn my focus to the scriptural truth that I know.

As you are learning God's word and lining up your thoughts with it you will see changes begin to happen in your life. It is a struggle but don't ever give up! This is a slow daily process that will change your life for the better. My hope is that this book will get you started down the faith-filled road that frees your mind.

Chapter One

Paying Attention

It is good to pay attention to the contents of the things that you eat, right? When you are buying packaged food items, do you stop and read the ingredients? If you are like me, you want to know how much sugar and other strange chemicals are in this thing that I am considering buying and how many calories it has.

On a road trip, things are different. I generally don't want to know what is inside the twinkie, beef jerky, or Snickers candy bar that I might buy for the trip. I might forget about what is inside all of the junk food at the gas station quick market and just eat the things that I like, yet I know are bad for me. But because I'm on a road trip going someplace fun, I make an exception for myself.

I have a friend, Terry, who would drive late at night from Los Angeles, California, to the mountains east of Phoenix, Arizona, non-stop. He would do it by slowly eating most of a ½ pound bag of peanut M&M's. He wouldn't eat all of them, but he did come close. Here is a driving hack: It is harder to fall asleep when you're driving if you're eating something.

You need to pay attention to what you put in your mouth. You also need to pay attention to what you put in your mind. Two things are true - what you put in your mouth can affect your heart and your other vital organs in the long term. What you put in your mind through your eyes and ears will affect how you feel and affect your *heart*, i.e. the core of your being.

In the Bible there are many words in both Hebrew and Greek that are translated as "mind." In the Old Testament, the Hebrew word *labab* is often translated "mind" or "heart." Sometimes the word heart refers to the actual physical organ in a person's chest, but many times it refers to the inner being—the seat of the will and the emotions.

In the New Testament, *kardia* is the Greek word for "heart," and it can also refer to the physical organ but is often translated as "mind" as well. The context makes all of the difference. This word for heart came to stand for both the rational and emotional elements in a person's life.

BRAIN vs. MIND

What is the difference between your brain and your mind? Your brain is the physical organ in your head, though it can't actually be touched, (except when one is having brain surgery.) It is made up of neurons and neurotransmitters. Perhaps you've heard someone say, "oh, he/she has a brain tumor." You may have also heard someone say, "you've lost your mind."

The mind is the ability to know something or to understand things. The mind refers to your thoughts, perceptions and your state of consciousness. And, by the way, you can't touch your mind either.

I found over 150 scriptures in the Bible with the word *mind* in them. Here is a small sample:

- Matthew 22:37 Jesus replied: "'Love the Lord your God with all your heart and with all your soul and with all your mind. (The gospel of Mark adds the word strength to this list.)
- Luke 24:38,45 38 Jesus said to them, "Why are you troubled, and why do doubts rise in your minds? 45 "Then he opened their minds so they could understand the Scriptures."
- Proverbs 23:7 KJV "As a man thinketh in his heart, so is he."
(Or so he becomes.)

Thoughts and Actions

You know this but let me say it – Our actions are a direct result of our thoughts.
For example, if you have a negative mind the first thing in the morning, when you wake up, you might think, "Oh God, it's morning, this is going to be a terrible day."

In her book *Battlefield of the Mind* Joyce Meyers says, "If you choose to think negative, counterproductive thoughts, nullifying thoughts, futile thoughts and vain thoughts then it should be no surprise to you that you will have a negative view of that day and perhaps of your life as well."

However, at that moment you can make a choice. You can *choose* to think and say something positive, edifying, and encouraging such as: *"This is the day the Lord has made. I WILL rejoice and be glad in it."* Psalm 118: 24.

By the choice of your will you are choosing to change your thinking. It's a struggle at first, but keep at it because it works. Keep at it because it is the truth, and it will set you free. It is important for you to hear yourself speak the truth out loud and it will reinforce right thinking.

Here is the truth – You cannot have a positive life and a negative mind. Did you know that the bible does not use the words positive and negative? It uses the words righteous and unrighteous, and they have much more weight and meaning to them than the words positive and negative. But if you begin to renew your mind according to God's word something will happen.

> Romans 12:2 "Do not conform any longer to the pattern of this world but be transformed by the renewing of your mind." (Here is the result as you renew your mind) "Then you will be able to test and approve what God's will is, his good, pleasing and perfect will." (For your life)

If you are struggling with a negative mind right now, please pause and pray, "Lord, I confess that I have been thinking unrighteous thoughts. Please forgive me. Please give me a renewed mind. I choose to rejoice and be glad."

Some of us have "stinking thinking" of which we need to rid ourselves. I want to encourage you to pray and tell the Lord that you want to move to higher ground spiritually. That you want to mature into the man/woman of God whom He has called you to be. Commit to agree with and cooperate with the Holy Spirit's promptings.

Until you get your mind on the right course, everything that you invest in it is going to slowly leak out and you won't change. This is why Psalm 118 is a good start. "This is the day the Lord has made I WILL be glad and rejoice." As an act of your will, you've decided to rejoice and be glad. You can be glad simply by choosing to think of your many blessings. Blessings like, I have food in my house and clean water. I have a place to live. I have a church family, etc.

Your Enemy

One of the tactics of the devil, however, is to tie up your mind with pettiness, anger and unforgiveness. As you come into this new season in your life you want to come in "headfirst," so to speak. What I mean by that is that when you can control your *head*, your thoughts, you can control the rest.

I have a silly example of controlling the "head." I was camping at the Eel River in northern California with friends. Their dog was playing in the water with all of us. I got out of the water and was all nice and dry and standing on the beach getting warm in the sunshine and talking with my friend. Suddenly his dog came out of the water and came directly toward us. You know what dogs do when they get out of the water, right? He started to shake all the water off of his fur. But I grabbed his head and he stopped instantly. Point: If you can control your head (mind) good things begin to happen.

There is a battle going on in your mind for control. In Ephesians 4 the apostle Paul gives us a plan of how to control our mind. It is called "put off" and "put on."

> Ephesians 4:22 – 24. "You were taught, with regard to your former way of life, to **put off** your old self, which is being corrupted by its deceitful desires; 23 to be made new in the attitude of your **minds**; 24 and to **put on** the new self, created to be like God in true righteousness and holiness."

By the power of the Holy Spirit in you, you can choose to think righteous God-honoring thoughts.

Chapter Two

Thought Bombs

Let me ask you a question. Can you control what you think about? We can't directly control our feelings, but we can control what we think about. And, if what we think doesn't reflect the truth, then what we feel doesn't reflect reality.

Suppose on Monday you heard a rumor at work that you were going to get laid off on Friday. Every day you would be getting more and more anxious. Suppose near quitting time on Thursday, you get a memo from your boss that he wants to see you at 10:00am on Friday.

You start thinking about your response if your boss is going to fire you. You start by thinking, "I'll hand in my resignation." Or "I'll wait and see" or "I'll tell him off." Then Friday comes and you are as nervous as a long-tailed cat in a room full of rocking chairs.

You nervously walk into the boss's office at 10:00 and all of the senior vice presidents are there and in unison they shout, *"Surprise! You've just been promoted to senior manager!*

When you thought that you were getting fired, what emotions did you have? However, your thoughts didn't conform to reality because what you believed didn't conform to reality.

> "The strong man is the one who is able to intercept at will the communication between the senses and the mind." *Napoleon Bonaparte*

The Devil

Jesus said the devil is a liar. That he is "the father of lies." (John 8:44). He lies to you and me about you and me. He tells us things about ourselves, other people, and circumstances that are just not true. He is a liar!

I call them thought bombs. The bible says, "take up the shield of faith, with which you can extinguish all the flaming arrows (thought bombs) of the evil one." Ephesians 6:16. The shield of faith is part of the armor of God that He provides for us, for our protection. The shield is the first barrier against the enemy's attacks. Faith recognizes the enemy's deceptive ploy and extinguishes the flaming arrow or thought bomb. It can happen like this – you are minding your own business at church and suddenly, a vile, dirty, and twisted thought pops into your mind. You may think, "where did that come from?" It is a thought bomb from the enemy.

Slowly, over the years, he keeps bombarding our minds with clever and nagging thoughts, suspicions, doubts and fears, theories and wonderings. He knows what bothers us most and our weak spots, and he patiently chips away at us. It is as though a video is stuck on replay in your mind to discourage you and distract you.

What to Do

Do not focus on the problem. Focus on the solution.

Have you ever tried this experiment? I did this in church one Sunday. I had a clear plastic pitcher of dark blue water representing polluted water. So, the question was, how to get rid of the dirty water – "the problem." I could focus on trying to splash out the "dirty water" or I could just pour more and more clean water into the pitcher until it overflows and washes out the dirty water.

Do not focus on the problem per se. Fill yourself up full to overflowing on Jesus and His Word. Fill up on worship and being in community in your church. Know this, that God inhabits the praise of His people (Psalm 22:3). Let that be your focus and priority and you will begin to wash away the problematic thinking.

We are in a battle. We know who the enemy is. We know where the battlefield is. So, how do we fight this battle in our mind and heart? How do we change? How do we change our thinking? How do we stop *stinking thinking*? What weapons do we have to fight this battle?

Powerful Weapons

In the next few chapters of this book, I am going to give you three powerful weapons that will help you fight the devil.

> 2 Corinthians 10:4–5. "The weapons we fight with are not the weapons of the world. On the contrary, they have divine power to demolish strongholds. [5] We demolish arguments and every pretension that sets itself up against the knowledge of God, and we take captive every thought to make it obedient to Christ."

Stronghold

Verse four uses the word "strongholds." What is a stronghold? The original Greek word means a fortified military stronghold. Here in 2 Corinthians, it is used figuratively to describe a false argument in which a person seeks shelter to escape reality. It is also used to describe a prison.

It is a mental habit. If you exercise a habit for long enough, for about six weeks or so, you will probably establish a stronghold. Moreover, a stronghold may also result from a series of actions and memories that are burned into your mind over time, or by the intensity of their traumatic impact.

Imagine a covered wagon from the pioneer days in America. The big wheels of the wagon would make a rut in the dirt road, a groove about the width of the wagon wheel. Because so many wagons had gone this way before, the person driving the wagon didn't really have to steer the wagon. The wagon just fell into the rut and went where it always went. The same thing happens with a stronghold – going and doing what you've always done.

Inferiority

For example, the feeling of inferiority is a stronghold. No one is born inferior to anyone else. You could be struggling with an inferiority complex if you keep getting the message from the enemy of your soul and the world around you that everyone else is smarter, faster, stronger and better looking than you are.

How do I change?

Know this - biblical change is initiated in your life through the regenerating power of the Holy Spirit!

"Biblical change," what does that mean? If you've surrendered your life to Jesus Christ, you're a new creation, empowered to make biblical changes in your life. Changes in your thoughts, and words. This also includes your actions.

One of the first things to do is to recognize that Biblical change is a continuing process. It is not a "one and done" type of thing. It is a reoccurring habit of *"putting off"* the old patterns of sin and then *"putting on"* the new practices of *right-wiseness* or righteousness.

> "You were taught, with regard to your former way of life, to **put off** your old self, which is being corrupted by its deceitful desires; 23 to be made new in the attitude of your minds; 24 and to **put on** the new self, created to be like God in true righteousness and holiness." Ephesians 4:22–24.

Righteousness is an attribute of God. It is a natural expression of His holiness. The righteousness of God means essentially the same as His faithfulness or truthfulness. That is, what is consistent with God's nature and promises. King David gives us a great sampling of things to think about and to praise God for in Psalms 103:

> 2 Praise the Lord, my soul,
> and forget not all his benefits—
> 3 who forgives all your sins
> and heals all your diseases,
> 4 who redeems your life from the pit
> and crowns you with love and compassion,
> 5 who satisfies your desires with good things so that your youth is renewed like the eagle's.

These things are right and true. These are the things that we want to put in our mind and heart to think about and practice.

So, we start by speaking the truth. Ephesians 4:15 says to "speak the truth in love." This is biblical change. What happens next? When we put these things in our mind, we find ourselves obeying Gods commands and directives in scripture in every area of our lives. Which comes down to our thoughts, our words, and our actions.

As You

These two words are significant – As you. As in **not** before. By cooperating with the Holy Spirit, you are stopping the old way of living by putting it off. Like taking off a dirty shirt. The Holy Spirit that lives inside you is alerting you to things what is not pleasing to God or good for you. We could say the old patterns of the old you. That is the old sinful patterns of how you used to handle life.

In Ephesians 4:25 we are told to put off falsehood or lying. Verse 28 instructs us put off stealing and unwholesome speech. In verse 29 we are told to put off bitterness, wrath, anger, clamor (crying, whining), slander, and malice.

Then, as you begin to **put on** the new practices of right-wiseness, guess what happens. You are renewed in the spirit and attitude of your mind.

PUT ON

What do we put on? As a righteous act before God, we begin by:

- Speaking the truth in love
- Stop stealing and start giving.
- Be a good worker.
- Speak to build other people up according to their need.
- Practice kindness, tenderness and forgiveness.

These are the things that you "put on." They are choices empowered by the Holy Spirit. You will find that in the tough decisions of life, *as you* choose what is godly and righteous you will grow and mature in the Lord.

As you choose to go God's way it is really an act of surrender. An act of yielding to the Holy Spirit's prompting. Here is a fact that may help you: You can't really surrender unless there is a battle. We know that there is a spiritual battle going on for the hearts and minds of every Christ follower.

As you yield to the Holy Spirit, He will show you what you need to repent from and immediately put aside. Things we need to stop doing. Did you know that we must learn to obey God's word? It doesn't just happen! There are things we need to stop saying and doing.

Tip - Don't do this slowly. When the Holy Spirit shows you something to stop, do it right away. The longer you wait the harder it is to obey.

First Weapon

The first weapon to battle the enemy of our soul is the Word of God! It's called the sword of the Spirit (Ephesians 6:17). Use it on the enemy! How? Speak it out loud. Speak the word. Have a few verses memorized to quote when the enemy attacks.

Some Examples:

> 1 Corinthians 10:13 "No temptation has overtaken you except what is common to mankind. And God is faithful; he will not let you be tempted/tested beyond what you can bear. But when you are tempted, he will also provide a way out so that you can endure it.
>
> 2 Corinthians 10:4–5 "The weapons we fight with are not the weapons of the world. On the contrary, they have divine power to demolish strongholds. 5 We demolish arguments and every pretension that sets itself up against the knowledge of God, and we take captive every thought to make it obedient to Christ."
>
> John 8:31-32 Jesus said, "If you hold to my teaching, you are really my

disciples. 32 Then you will know the truth, and the truth will set you free."

Philippians 4:13 "I can do all this through him (Christ) who gives me strength."

If you'll continue to study God's word you **will** know the truth and the truth **will** set you free.

As you do this God will reveal things to you about *you* and that you must face and not deny. Something God showed me recently was just how selfish I am and how judgmental I can be. *Ouch*.

The truth is always revealed through God's word. Sadly, we don't always accept it or act upon it. It is a painful process to face our faults and shortcomings and to deal with them.

Generally, I think that we try to justify our misbehavior. We say things like, "that's how I was raised." We allow our past to negatively affect the rest of our lives. Our past may explain why we are suffering, but we must not use it as an excuse to stay in bondage. To stay stuck in a stronghold.

And so, we are all without excuse because Jesus always stands ready to fulfill His promise and to set the captive free. He will help us to victory if we are willing to go all the way through with Him.

The Way Out

1 Corinthians 10:13 Amplified. "[13]For no temptation (no trial regarded as enticing to sin), (no matter how it comes or where it leads) has overtaken you and laid hold on you that is not common to man (that is, no temptation or trial has come to you that is beyond human resistance and that is not adjusted and adapted and belonging to human experience, and such as man can bear). But God is faithful (to His Word and to His compassionate nature), and He (can be trusted) not to let you be tempted and tried and assayed beyond your ability and strength of resistance and power to endure, but with the temptation He will (always) also provide the way out (the means of escape to a landing place), that you may be capable and strong and powerful to bear up under it patiently."

We Have Weapons

We have weapons to tear down strongholds. God doesn't abandon us and leave us helpless. 1 Corinthians 10:13 states that God promises us that He will not allow us to be tempted beyond what we can bear, but with every temptation/trial he'll provide a way out.

The battle is in our mind; that is, in our thoughts and attitudes. We know that our outward behavior is the result of our inner life. The devil knows that if he can plant selfish unrighteous thoughts in our mind, then our actions will follow.

You may have some stronghold in your life that needs to be broken. Let me say that there is a battle and God is on your side. The good news is that God is fighting for you.

I started this book by saying we need to pay attention to the contents of what is inside that *twinkie*. I said to pay attention to what you are allowing into your mind. Here is a tip that will help you every day.

Tip

It's good to pay attention to the contents before you put something in your mouth, or in your mind. When God tells us what it means to make Jesus the Lord of our thoughts and of our mind, He puts it this way in Philippians 4:8, "Whatever is true, whatever is noble, whatever is right, whatever is pure, whatever is lovely, whatever is admirable - if anything is excellent or praiseworthy - **think** about such things."

That is God's diet plan for your heart and mind. And notice the deciding factor isn't whether you should watch something or listen to something or read something in general, it is the particular content!

Not if it's funny, not if it's clever, not if it's entertaining. Not if you like the beat, not if it's something "everyone" is seeing or

18

listening to, or it is in the top forty. And not if you like the style.

Over 40

If you are over 40 years old, you can't afford to eat any old thing that you want. Why not? Because you could have an early date with a heart specialist or even an undertaker. You must decide based on whether the contents of this tasty treat are healthy or unhealthy for you.

That's how your Savior wants you to decide what you read, listen to or watch. Look at the contents. Think about some of your TV programs and/or your favorite music, YouTube, Instagram, the books you read, the humor you listen to, and the movies you see.

Does it pass God's test for what gets into your heart and mind?

- Is it something to be admired?
- Is what it says or shows pure?
- Is it something with which Jesus would feel comfortable?
- Is it something He would laugh at, and He would recommend?
- Does it portray God's ways or sinful ways?
- Is it innocent or is it suggestive?
- Is it positive or negative?

God cares about what you're "eating" mentally. He makes it very clear.

He says:

> Proverbs 4:23 "Above all else, guard your heart because it is the wellspring of life."
>
> 2 Corinthians 10:5 "We demolish arguments and every pretension that sets itself up against the knowledge of God, and we take captive every thought to make it obedient to Christ."

We're in a battle – so fight! God is on your side.

Chapter Three

Weapons for Battle

If you are a Christ follower, your Christian walk is a direct result of what you believe.

We said you cannot have a positive life and a negative mind. A negative or unrighteous mind is what we call *stinking thinking*. So, we want to get rid of "stinking thinking."

We have discovered that we are in a spiritual battle as well. We know who the enemy is, and we know where the battlefield is. The battlefield is in our mind. So, how do we fight this battle? What weapons do we have to fight with?

We have a weapon that we must use to fight the battle in our mind and to fight the evil one. We must fight the negative, unrighteous, sexually charged, selfish and godless input that we receive from the world as well.

Weapon

The weapon that we have is the Bible, the sword of the Spirit. It is the living, active, precious and powerful Word of God. It has divine power to demolish strongholds and arguments and every pretension that sets

itself up against the knowledge of God.
(2 Corinthians 10:4)

Psalm 19 tells us that the word of God is "perfect, right, pure and firm."

> 2 Timothy 3:16-17 "16 All Scripture is God-breathed and is useful for teaching, rebuking, correcting and training in righteousness, 17 so that the servant of God may be thoroughly equipped for every good work."

I think we, as liberated affluent Americans, (if you live in America) take the Holy Scriptures for granted. We may have four or five hardcopies of the Bible in our home. We may even have one propping up that old velvet picture of Elvis Presley. If you live in America, Bibles are inexpensive. Publishers are coming out with new cover designs every year. Increasingly there are a variety of versions and translations from which to pick. Plus, we have Bible apps on our smart phones and computers.

As a side note, there is a question that I get asked occasionally. "What is the difference between a translation and a version?" There are numerous versions and a few translations. A translation is from the original language into your language. A version of the Bible is another rendering of that translation. I could write a whole page about the different translations available but that is another book.

The Word of God is Precious

There is a video on YouTube of the Kimyal tribe in western Papua New Guinea receiving the printed Word of God in their own language for the very first time. It is amazing! I would encourage you to watch it. Here is the link: https://www.youtube.com/watch?v=ag2AzWgRKAk

The Kimyal people are sustenance framers who were untouched by the outside world until World Team missionaries Phillip and Phyllis Masters brought the gospel in 1963. Phil was martyred in 1968 with fellow missionary Stan Dale. They were killed and cannibalized by the Yale tribe. Fifty years later they have the New Testament in their language! Please watch the video and see how they treasure the Word of God.

The Word of God is precious and powerful – **Read it, Study it, Share it.** This is how we fight the battle in our mind. "As a man thinks in his heart, so is he..." Proverbs 23:7.

We're In a Battle

We are in a battle – so **fight**! Don't drop your guard and don't give up. Here's the thing, as you stay in the Word of God and let the Spirit of God freshen your inner man, you'll stay more alert to the schemes of the devil. The word of God has a direct effect on your mind – healing it. It is easy to give up in a battle because there is resistance.

Because it is uphill and hard. It seems like everyone else is going in the other direction.

Understand this, it takes faith to go on through. It takes faith to *keep on keeping on*. In her book *Battlefield of the Mind,* Joyce Meyers says, "you will never see the end if you give up in the middle."

We need to encourage one another in the battle. This is why being in the community of your local Bible teaching church is so critical. You are not in this battle alone. You can tell your friend in your small group, "Don't give up and *keep on, keeping on.* Keep doing the right thing." And they can tell you the same thing, and you can pray for one another.

> "Let us not become weary in doing good, for at the proper time we will reap a harvest *if* we do not give up." Galatians. 6:9

What does this mean and what do we do? Continue to act nobly and do what is right even when it is difficult. Then at the appointed season you will reap a harvest. There will be a beneficial return to you. But don't loosen your grip. Don't relax your courage. Keep breathing in the Spirit of God and you won't faint. As you struggle through the difficult times in a God honoring way, you will grow spiritually. It is like following through on a commitment you made even when it is inconvenient and maybe even painful. Following through on commitments matures you.

I Wonder Why

Have you ever wondered why you struggle with sinful thoughts and why you say some awful, even filthy things? Why do we do some hurtful and damaging things especially to those closest to us?

It all started with Adam and Eve in the Garden of Eden, in Genesis chapter three. Adam and God had a relationship. What I mean is that Adam knew God. They spent time together and spoke to one another. However, through Adam's disobedience that relationship was shattered. He was out of sync with God. It had a negative effect on his mind as well. He and Eve lost their true perception of reality and the idea of "knowing" was no longer relational.

If you remember from Genesis, they tried to hide from God. How silly. God is omnipresent. Because God is omnipresent no one can hide from Him. Their disobedience distorted their perception of reality and their ability to think clearly.

Through the residual effects of their disobedience, we inherited spiritual death. We are now born into sin (Romans 5:12).

When they disobeyed God, what happened to them spiritually? They died. This is commonly called The Fall. Their union with God was severed and they were separated from God.

God specifically said: "You must not eat from the tree of the knowledge of good and evil, for when you eat of it you will surely die." Genesis 2:17

Did they die physically? Not right away, though physical death is a result of the fall. They died spiritually. They were separated from God's presence and were physically thrown out of the garden. See Genesis 3:24.

In essence, when Adam and Eve sinned, they lost a true knowledge of God. In God's original design, knowledge was relational. That's the idea behind the Hebrew concept of knowledge – intimate personal relationship.

Data

To our modern world, knowledge is merely a collection of data. That kind of "knowledge" can make someone arrogant. A person may know some data, and some trivia but they have no experience to go with it.

The Fall distorted Adam and Eve's perception of reality. They were, shall we say, darkened in their understanding. As a result, they became fearful and anxious.

Did you know that the first emotion expressed by fallen mankind was fear? See Genesis 3:10.

In the Genesis account we now see fear and anxiety. We see it in Adam's son, Cain. We also we see depression and anger.

> Genesis 4:5–7 "Why are you angry? Why is your face downcast? If you do what is right, will you not be accepted? But if you do not do what is right, sin is crouching at the door; its desire is to have you, but you must master it."

Why was Cain angry and depressed? Because he didn't do what was right.

It's been said that, "You don't feel your way into good behavior; you behave your way into good feelings."

> Jesus said it this way – "If you know these things, you are blessed if you do them." John. 13:17

Adam and Eve's sin affected their will to choose. Prior to the fall, while in the garden, they could make only one wrong choice. Everything else they wanted was okay except eating from the tree of the knowledge of good and evil. A whole bunch of good choices and only one bad choice. ONE!

Choose

You know what happened. The choice they made has affected each one of us. You and I are confronted every day with choices. Hopefully we make more good choices than bad ones.

Apart from the Holy Spirit in your life, the greatest power you possess is the power to choose.

You can choose to:

- Go to church or not
- To Pray or not
- To read your Bible or not
- To bless others or not
- You can choose to walk according to the flesh or according to the Spirit

    Romans 8:5 "Those who live according to the sinful nature have their <u>minds</u> set on what that nature desires; but those who live in accordance with the Spirit have their <u>minds</u> set on what the Spirit desires."

    Romans 8:5 Amplified Bible
    "For those who are according to the flesh and are controlled by its unholy desires set their <u>minds</u> on and pursue those things which gratify the flesh, but those who are according to the Spirit and are controlled by the desires of the Spirit set their <u>minds</u> on and seek those things which gratify the (Holy) Spirit."

    Deuteronomy 30: 19
    "This day I call heaven and earth as witnesses against you that I have set before you life and death, blessings and curses. Now <u>choose</u> life, so that you and your children may live."

Dear Ones – Choose LIFE!

Your life may be in a state of chaos currently because of years of wrong thinking, and of having a wrong mindset. Your life will not get straightened out until your mind gets straightened out.

You must tear down strongholds and patterns of thinking that have been built up in your mind and are destroying you.

Here's how: You start by fully surrendering your life to Jesus Christ. Repent of your sins and believe on Jesus. Ask Him to forgive you and to come into your heart and save you. Salvation is a free gift.

You can't earn it by being good. It is free but it will cost you your life.

Next, use the precious powerful Word of God to wash your mind. The Word of God is a powerful weapon. We must purposely choose right thinking and continue to choose right thoughts that line up with God's word.

Study these scriptures from Phil. 4:6-9:

> "Do not be anxious about anything, but in every situation, by prayer and petition, with thanksgiving, present your requests to God. 7 And the peace of God, which transcends all understanding, will guard your hearts and your minds in Christ Jesus. 8 Finally, brothers and sisters, whatever

is true, whatever is noble, whatever is right, whatever is pure, whatever is lovely, whatever is admirable—if anything is excellent or praiseworthy—*think* about such things. 9 Whatever you have learned or received or heard from me or seen in me—put it into practice. And the God of peace will be with you."

When the scripture directs us to "think about such things" you must ask yourself what things are true, noble, right and pure. Scripture fits this description perfectly.

May I suggest that you memorize the verses above, as well as others that I've cited. These verses are like arrows in your quiver to shoot down the negative unrighteous thoughts that often plague you.

Chapter Four

Next Weapon

Ask God for help and ask often. You can't overcome your situation by determination alone. You need to be determined, but determined in the Holy Spirit and not your own flesh. The Holy Spirit is your helper so seek His help. Lean on Him, as it were. Ask, and cry out to the Lord.

Have you ever prayed a prayer like this: "Oh God, if you don't help me, I don't know if I am going to make it." Or "Oh God, if you don't help me, I won't be the husband/wife you want me to be." Or "Oh God, Oh God without your help I don't know how to be the parent you want me to be." Pray, cry out to Him. Open your heart to Him and be honest.

Praying aloud to the Lord and saying biblical things to God out loud like, "I am in Christ, God's word is true, the devil is a liar." Or "I will rejoice and be glad." Or "I declare I am free!" Expect God to do good in your life. Speak these things in faith believing.

> Proverbs 18:21 "The tongue has the power of life and death, and those who love it will eat its fruit..."

Say this loudly – **"God is on my side. He loves me. He is helping me!"**

Thoughts and Words

Our thoughts become our words. So, we must choose life-giving thoughts and our words will follow.

When the battle seems like it's not going to stop and you think, "I'll never make it," remember that we are changing the way we think, away from a worldly mindset and learning to think like Jesus does.

- Impossible – No!
- Difficult – Yes!

You're working with God to reprogram your mind. As you know, your mind is sort of like a computer, only faster. As you keep cooperating with Him and putting righteous things in your mind you start to think differently – biblically. Talk to Him often and don't give up.

It's a little bit by a little bit. This reprogramming, if you will, takes time.

So don't be discouraged if your progress is slow. When Moses and the Jews left the slavery of Egypt, they did not go straight into the Promise Land. These people had been enslaved for generations (400 years). These former slaves may have been out of Egypt, but the slavery mindset was not out of them. So, they wandered in the wilderness for forty years until it was time to go into the Promise Land. This was kind of like forty years of reality therapy as God was preparing them for the Promise Land.

Notice that before the Israelites could possess the Promise Land, they had to drive out the occupying enemies – little by little. Take note of this, they were in the Promise Land, but they still had enemies to fight.

A pastor said – "inch by inch anything is a cinch." The same is true with your thinking.

The Devil

The devil will work overtime to stop you from renewing your mind. He knows that his influence in your mind is finished once you choose the right thoughts and reject wrong ones.

The devil will try to deflate you, discourage you and distract you. Discouragement destroys hope. So, this will be one of the things the devil will try to do. He will tell you that you are hopeless. And without hope, you give up, which is what the devil wants you to do. It all starts with your thoughts.

When discouragement and condemnation try to overtake your mind do this spot check: Ask yourself, *what am I thinking about?* Take a good look at your thought life and think about what you are thinking about. I am saying that you cannot live effectively and joyously without right thinking.

Maybe the lie the devil is whispering to you sounds like this: "I'm not going to make it; this is too hard. I always fail, nothing ever changes." Or "I'm tired of trying. I pray but I don't think God hears me." Or "God probably won't answer my prayer because he is disappointed in how I've been acting. I am so unworthy"

Let me ask you a question: If you think discouraging thoughts all day long, how will you feel at the end of the day?

Instead of thinking unrighteous thoughts or negative thoughts try saying this to yourself:

"*W***ell, things are going slow; but thank God I'm making progress. I'm sure glad I'm on the right path. Yesterday was a tough day. I chose wrong thinking. Father in heaven please forgive me and help me to keep on keeping on. This is a new day. I love you, Lord, and You love me. Your mercies are new every morning. I refuse to be discouraged."**

Say this: "I believe God is working in me no matter how I feel or what the situation looks like. The Lord has begun a good work in me, and He will bring it to full completion**."**

Don't quit. Continue by faith and not by feeling.

The television personality Regis Philben once said, "When you get knocked down, get up, show up and some people you'll cheer up."

34

Truth

When the devil tries to condemn you, use your Word weapon and quote Romans 8:1, "There is no condemnation for those who are in Christ Jesus."

Here is the truth, God **is** delivering you little by little, so be patient with yourself.

When you fail, which you will because none of us are 100% yet, it doesn't mean you're a failure. It means you don't do everything right. Your success or shall I say your victory will come in due time and at the right season, so don't receive the condemnation the devil throws at you.

A Righteous Mind

A righteous mind, or we could say a positive mind, will always produce faith and hope. An unrighteous mind, or a negative mind, always produces fear and doubt.

Some people are afraid to hope because they have been hurt in life. There have been serious disappointments in their lives. So, they avoid hoping, and this can set up a negative life.

Many of God's people know Romans 8:28, "We know that in all things God works for the good of those who love him and are called according to his purposes." This scripture doesn't say that *all* things are good, but it does say that God works for the good *in* all things.

Let's say you get in your car to go to the store, or shopping with your best friend or you are going to go fishing with a buddy, but your car won't start.

There are two ways that you can look at this situation:

1. "I knew it. It never fails. Every time I want to do something, it gets all messed up. My plans always flop."
2. Or, say, "Well I wanted to go to the store/fishing, but it looks like I can't now. I'll go later when the car is fixed. In the meantime, I believe this change in plans is going to work out for good. There is a reason why I need to be home so I'm going to enjoy it."

When things do not go according to your plans, can you feel your emotions getting all stirred up? Anytime you don't get what you want, do your feelings rise up and try to get you to go into a self-pity mode and then to go negative? Or can you adjust to the situation and enjoy the day, rather than choosing to be irritable?

Even a positive person doesn't have everything go their way. But they can decide to enjoy themselves no matter what happens.

Going Negative

The negative person never enjoys anything.

An extremely negative person can walk into someone's home that has been completely remodeled and painted, etc. and rather saying how great it looks they see a smudge on the wall and a chip on the coffee table.

Please hear me, if you're a negative person, please don't feel condemned. The pathway to freedom starts when we face the problem without making excuses for it. Are you self-aware enough to be honest with yourself and admit, *I'm negative.* If so, then say this, "I want to change."

There are always reasons why someone is negative. But if you're a Christ follower you are a new person. "Therefore, if anyone is in Christ, he is a new creation; the old has gone, the new has come!" (1 Corinthians 5:17

You are a New Creation.

You don't have to allow the old things that happened to you keep on affecting your life in Christ. You can have your mind renewed according to God's Word. If you want to change, ask the Holy Spirit to convict and convince you when you go negative. *Each and every time.*

John 16 tells us that it is the Holy Spirit's job to convict us of sin and unrighteousness. When conviction comes you must confess whatever it is to the Lord and ask him to help you. This is how you lean on the Lord.

Abraham

> Romans 4:18-20 "Against all hope, Abraham in hope believed and so became the father of many nations, just as it had been said to him, "So shall your offspring be." [19] Without weakening in his faith, he faced the fact that his body was as good as dead—since he was about a hundred years old—and that Sarah's womb was also dead. [20] Yet he did not waver through unbelief regarding the promise of God but was strengthened in his faith and gave glory to God."

Be ready to receive what God has for you.

You may have imagined your life a certain way by now, but things have happened, and your choices or someone else's choices have brought you to where you are today.

For some of you, things happened *to you* that were out of your control, awful things, and wrong things. Maybe a broken engagement, a lost job, sickness, divorce, abuse or a death.

Nevertheless, you are right here, right now.

Believe

We can believe God for many things. But beyond all of them we believe in Someone – JESUS CHRIST. We don't always know what is going to happen. We just know it is all going to work out for our good and His glory.

As you and I choose righteous or positive thoughts, I think we'll be more in the flow of God. Or shall I say, flowing with Him.

You may be thinking: "Pastor Dan, you don't know my circumstances." You're right, I don't. But God does. Believe that He is working on your behalf.

Remember Romans 4:18. Abraham is sizing up the situation regarding his age and Sarah's age. He didn't ignore the facts. The Bible says, "He considered (thought about) the impotence of his body and the barrenness of Sarah's dead womb." Although all human reason for hope was gone, he hoped in faith.

You could say that Abraham was very positive about a very negative situation.

Hebrews 6:19 tells us that hope is the "anchor of the soul." Hope is a force that keeps us steady in the storm and in times of trial.

Don't ever stop hoping. If you do, you'll have a miserable life. If you already have a miserable life, start hoping.

Don't be afraid! Expect God to work in your life and to do a miracle.

A prayer to consider: If you have a sour attitude and a negative mind, pray this: "LORD, I admit that I have a negative mind and I confess that to you. Please forgive me. Help me, remind me to choose righteous godly thoughts. Lord, I want to be someone who is expecting to hear from you and to see you move in my life. Be the strength of my life. My hope is in you!"

Chapter Five

SO, FIGHT!

Changing how we think is a battle. We've said that the transformation of our mind is a slow but progressive process. It is inch by inch. We're in a fight and the battlefield is in our mind. My admonition to you is to fight!

It is impossible to get from wrong behavior to right behavior without first changing our thoughts. Have you noticed that the *fighting* has gotten more sophisticated, more advanced, more insidious, more brutal and vicious than ever?

The Battle

What do we know? We realize that we're in a spiritual battle. We know where the battlefield is. It is in our mind. We know who the enemy is.

> Ephesians 6:12 "For our struggle is not against flesh and blood, but against the rulers, against the authorities, against the powers of this dark world and against the spiritual forces of evil in the heavenly realms."

Jesus said the devil is a liar (John 8:44). He lies to you and me about you and me. He also has a strategy. In her book *Battlefield of the Mind,* Joyce Meyers says that the devil's strategy is to bombard our minds with "cleverly devised patterns of little nagging thoughts, suspicions, doubts, fears, wonderings, reasoning and theories."

A passive person may want to do the right thing, but unless they purposely activate their mind and line it up with God's word, they will not do the right thing.

A friend may come to you for prayer and say "I have a problem with lust. I just can't seem to stay away from the opposite sex. Will you pray for my deliverance?" The Holy Spirit may give you a bit of insight and you say, "Yes, I'll pray for you, but you must be accountable because you are allowing it to play on the screen in your mind. You can't visualize pornographic pictures in your mind or imagine yourself with other people if you ever what to enjoy freedom."

We're in a battle. You can't be passive if you want to experience breakthroughs in your life. This person who comes to you seeking help wants to be free. In other words, they want a change in their behavior but not their thinking.

The mind is often the area where we play around with sin. The way for sinful action is paved by sinful thinking.

The Truth Weapon

What weapons do we have to fight this battle? As we said in the previous chapter, the first weapon is the Word of God. Your Bible. The powerful, precious, holy word of God. I implore you to read it daily, study it, and commit key passages to memory because it will help your mind. Memorize? You say, "I can't remember anything." Let me say that the person who says that they can't and the person that says that they can, are both right. You can do what you set your mind to do.

Dealing with Satan is not a power encounter, it is a truth encounter. When we expose his lie with God's truth, his power is broken.

God's word is truth!

That's why Jesus said, "*You shall know the truth and the truth shall set you free.*"

> John 17:15 (Jesus' prayer) "My prayer is not that you take them out of the world but that you protect them from the evil one. Sanctify them by the truth; your word is truth."

This is why the first piece of armor that the apostle Paul mentions in Ephesians 6 to stand against the schemes of the devil is *the belt of truth*. Satan's lie cannot withstand the truth any more than darkness can withstand the light of the sun.

We're not called to chase out the darkness, rather we are called to turn on the light!

Renewing Your Mind

We renew our mind by filling it with God's word. According to Philippians 4:7, "Let the peace of God rule in your heart and mind." As you continue to fill up your mind with God's truth, you will equip yourself to recognize the lie and take it captive and cast it aside.

Prayer

The second weapon we have in our powerful arsenal is prayer. Simply talking to God. A good practice is to take the word of God with you into prayer. Pray scripture back to God. Remind Him of His promises. Listen for the Holy Spirit's still small voice. A gentle whisper as it were. You can ask the Holy Spirit how to pray as well. If you have a spiritual language, pray in the spirit; it will build up your inner man.

I can tell you that praying out loud is powerful! It is so helpful to hear yourself speaking the truth about your situation. And because spiritual warfare is in your mind coming at you as "thought bombs" it is very helpful to pray aloud, to get out of your head, so to speak.

> Ephesians 6:13-18 "Therefore put on the full armor of God, so that when the day of evil comes, you may be able to stand your ground, and after you have done everything, to stand. [14] Stand firm then, with the belt

> of truth buckled around your waist, with the breastplate of righteousness in place, [15] and with your feet fitted with the readiness that comes from the gospel of peace. [16] In addition to all this, take up the shield of faith, with which you can extinguish all the flaming arrows of the evil one. [17] Take the helmet of salvation and the sword of the Spirit, which is the word of God. [18] And *pray* in the Spirit on all occasions with all kinds of prayers and requests. With this in mind, be alert and always keep on praying for all the saints."

We're in a battle. The battlefield is our mind. That is where we are attacked. We must rebuke the enemy in the name of Jesus.

In his book *Bondage Breakers* Dr. Neil Andreson says, "The devil is under no obligation to obey your thoughts." He is not omnipresent like the Lord. So, we rebuke him out loud. When under attack don't just *think* your rebuke – *Say it out loud!*

I had a demonic encounter one night while I was ministering in Fiji. It was raining outside, and I was asleep in the pastor's home. Suddenly I felt a slight touch on my chest. I opened my eyes and saw what looked like a black silk scarf sort of swaying about. I sat up and instantly I knew it was demonic. Out loud I said, "I rebuke you in Jesus' name, get out of here." It left immediately. I laid back down and I was literally vibrating for a moment. Outside the rain and the wind got more violent and loud for a few minutes and then it was quiet.

The point of telling you this is to understand that when the enemy attacks you must deal with him out loud and in Jesus' name.

Third Weapon is Praise

What is praise? It is the verbally thanking, honoring, glorifying and adoring God. We worship God by praise. In our relationship with Him we have seen and known His character. We have seen how He operates, and we say it out loud.

Prayer is talking to God is the first person. For example, you can say something like this from your heart: "God, you are so faithful, and you never change. You're the same yesterday, today and forever. Thank you for your provision and blessing. Thank you for your mercy. Your mercy is new every morning. God you are so holy and pure and right."

Thoughtful, heartfelt praise and worship of God heightens your awareness of Him and His love for you.

What does verbal praise do for you?

Spiritually: When you verbally praise God, it drives the devil away. The devil can't stand it. The Bible says that God inhabits the praises of His people.

> Psalm 147:1 "Praise the Lord. How good it is to sing praises to our God, how pleasant and fitting to praise him!"

Follow this injunction:

> Psalm 100:4 "Enter his gates with thanksgiving and into his courts with praise."

As we do this we are in His presence. When you're in a battle you want His presence. You want Jesus right there fighting for you.

Physically: Singing your praise activates both sides of your brain. When you open your mouth and press out the old air in your lungs as you are singing you get more oxygen to your brain and body.

The experts tell us that singing boosts your immune system. After a 60-minute rehearsal of Mozart's Requiem they found that concentrations of immunoglobin A - proteins in the immune system which function as antibodies - and hydrocortisone - an anti-stress hormone, increased significantly during the rehearsal.

This is different than merely listening to music. Listening to music is good but it does not have the same physiological boost that singing does.

Many studies have focused on the health benefits of singing, and the evidence is overwhelming. Google it and see what you will find. Here is what Professor Graham Welch, Director of Educational Research, University of Surrey, Roehampton, UK found:

- Singing releases endorphins into your system and makes you feel energized and uplifted. People who sing are healthier than people who don't.
- Singing gives the lungs a workout.
- Singing tones abdominal and intercostals muscles and the diaphragm and stimulates circulation.
- Singing makes us breathe more deeply than some forms of strenuous exercise, so we take in more oxygen, improve aerobic capacity, and experience a release of muscle tension as well.

How does vocal praise affect the believer?

When we praise God, we are acknowledging that it is not our own efforts that produce blessings and prosperity. In Deuteronomy 7 and 8, the children of Israel are told to remember to thank God for the abundance they have received. It was God, not their own efforts, that gave them wealth.

The other thing that praising God and giving thanks to God does, is that it helps to keep us humble. It is much easier for God to work with you when you are humble. He can't work with someone that is full of pride.

Did you know that any time we operate in a high degree of faith, that praise and thankfulness are there?

> Colossians 2:6 7 " So then, just as you received Christ Jesus as Lord, continue to live in him, [7] rooted and built up in him, strengthened in the faith as you were taught, and overflowing with thankfulness."

When you are believing and asking God for something and it is completed, praise and thanksgiving are a natural response. What some people often neglect is how they can increase their faith with praise and worship.

Here is what happens. By focusing on your problems instead of praising God, you become self-centered and even prideful. Praise forces or pushes you to get your attention on God and off of your problems. I say this in my church, "Your problems are only around you; God is over you. Take your eyes off the horizon and lift them vertically toward heaven."

Some people say that they are praying, but they are super focused on their problems. So, what they are really doing is just complaining. If you focus on the Word of God, faith will come.

> Philippians 4:4 "Rejoice in the Lord always: and again, I say, Rejoice."
>
> Hebrews 13:15 "Through Jesus, therefore, let us continually offer to God a sacrifice of praise, the fruit of lips that confess his name."

In this verse, praising God is represented as a sacrificial offering. Put self aside and praise the Lord. Don't let pride get in your way. Take charge of your thoughts and feelings and begin to speak praise to God and give thanks, even if there are no emotions to go with it.

Doxo

Sometimes we need help with what to say as we praise and thank the Lord. Here is some help.

> 1 Peter 2:9 "But you are a chosen people, a royal priesthood, a holy nation, a people belonging to God, that you may declare the praises of him who called you out of darkness into his wonderful light."

The word glory in Greek is *Doxo*. It means to say something good about, or you have a good opinion about someone. In this case, God.

Here is the hymn entitled *Doxology*:

"Praise God for whom all blessings flow; Praise Him all creatures here below. Praise Him above ye heavenly host; praise Father, Son and Holy Ghost, Amen."

Sing this to the Lord every day.

Weapons

Three powerful weapons to do battle with:

1. The Word of God. Reading it, studying it, memorizing it and sharing it.
2. Prayer. Talking to God and asking for His help and intervention
3. Praise. Worshipping God with our voice and our way of life

If you want to live the life that Jesus provides, then seek that new powerful life by setting your mind and keeping it set on things above and not on things of earth.

> Colossians 3:1-2. "Since then, you have been raised with Christ, set your *hearts* on things above, where Christ is seated at the right hand of God. ² Set your *minds* on things above, not on earthly things."

If you want a good life, then you must keep your mind on good things.

Some of us want a good life but we are passively sitting around wishing something good would happen to us. Sometimes we are even jealous of friends and acquaintances who are living in victory. There are good godly things happening in their lives.

If you desire success and victory over your problems, if you want to live the resurrection life, you've got to have a backbone and not just a wishbone. You must be active and not passive. Right action begins with right thinking. Don't be passive in your mind. Start today to choose the right thoughts.

Your Will

By an act of your will choose to have a righteous/positive outlook. Like really believing that God is good. Say to yourself, "God is good. I will rejoice and be glad in him." It is a daily challenge to maintain that attitude. One thing that is very helpful is to have righteous and Christ honoring positive conversations with your friends and family.

Echo this scripture aloud today, "I *will* declare your name to my brothers; in the presence of the congregation, I *will* sing your praises." And again, "*I will* put my trust in him."
(Hebrews 2:12)

I will.

Chapter Six

The Normal Mind

To change the way you think is a challenging and slow process. As a committed Christ follower, it **is** happening – inch by inch and day by day. God is healing your mind.

So far, we've said that biblical change is initiated in your life through the amazing power of the Holy Spirit. You are empowered to make godly changes in your thoughts, your words and your actions. However, it all starts with your mind.

It also comes by believing God's word and speaking God's word. It comes by believing and obeying God's word.

> "Then you will know the truth and the truth will set you free." John 8:32

> "He sent forth his word and healed them; he rescued them from the grave." Psalms 107:20

As you are reading this, have you felt a struggle or a conflict in your mind? Old habit patterns and certain ways of thinking are hard to break. Know this, as you choose between good and evil, righteous and unrighteous, positive and negative thinking, there will be a struggle. You are normal.

If you have set your mind and your heart to please God and not yourself, there will be a bit of pain, because self or your flesh, wants what it wants. By the way, no one can do this for you. It must be your choice.

> Romans 8:5 "Those who live according to the sinful nature have their *mind set* on what that nature desires; *but* those who live in accordance with the spirit have their *mind set* on what the spirit desires." (emphasis added)

Renewing your mind is the process by which your thoughts and your will become more and more Christlike. You can see it in your increasing faithfulness to God and obedience to His word. Renewal of your mind is a daily thing.

> Ephesians 4:23 "Be renewed in the attitude of your mind."

Biblical thinking

What do I mean by biblical thinking? Here is what the apostle Paul said:

> Colossians 3:1-2 "Since, then, you have been raised with Christ, *set your hearts* on things above, where Christ is seated at the right hand of God. ² *Set your minds* on things above, not on earthly things."
>
> Philippians 4:8-9 "Finally, brothers, whatever is true, whatever is noble,

> whatever is right, whatever is pure, whatever is lovely, whatever is admirable—if anything is excellent or praiseworthy—*think about such things.* ⁹ Whatever you have learned or received or heard from me or seen in me, put it into practice. And the God of peace will be with you."

From these two passages we learn that we must set our mind on spiritual things. What are those things? This passage in Philippians tells us what to think about. Think about what is true, pure, lovely, noble and admirable. Such as thinking and meditating on God's word.

Think about passages of scripture that you have memorized. If you have children, think about how much you love them. You can think about other pure and noble things, like those things from which God has saved you. That He pulled you out of the darkness and brought you into His marvelous light. Think about the fact that He has given you hope and a future.

Question: What is the condition of your mind today?

Have you noticed that the condition of your mind changes? One day your mind is calm and serene and the next day it is anxious and fearful. Or you decide something and think that you're "in the clear" only to find yourself later confused about it. For me there are times when I can believe God for things, and other times when doubt and unbelief haunts me without mercy.

Normal Mind

So, what is a normal mind? If we know what "normal" is, we can deal with, shall we say, an abnormal mind or unrighteous thinking.

Would you say that for a growing Christ follower that a critical, faultfinding, judgmental, and suspicious mind should be considered abnormal? Maybe I just described your thought life for the past few months. Our minds are not *born again* with our new birth experience, they must be renewed.

> Romans 12:2 "Do not conform any longer to the pattern of this world but be transformed by the *renewing* of your mind. Then you will be able to test and approve what God's will is—his good, pleasing and perfect will."

Renewal is a process that requires time. Satan will aggressively fight against the renewal of your mind. And because of that I want to remind you to FIGHT! We're in a battle, so press on. The Holy Spirit has empowered you to gain control of your thought life.

So, when is your mind normal? Is it supposed to wander all over? Should you be able to keep focused on what you're doing? Should your mind be upset and confused, or should it be peaceful, with you being reasonably sure of the direction you're taking?

Worry, Doubt, Fear

What about worry, unbelief, doubt and fear? The Bible teaches us that we should have the mind of Christ.

> Ephesians 1:17–18. "I keep asking that the God of our Lord Jesus Christ, the glorious Father, may give you the Spirit of wisdom and revelation, so that you may know him better. [18] I pray also that the eyes of your heart may be enlightened in order that you may know the hope to which he has called you, the riches of his glorious inheritance in the saints,"

"The eyes of your heart." What is that? It is your mind. According to the Bible, the mind and the spirit work together.

What does the mind do, what does the spirit do?

> 1 Corinthians 2:11 "For who among men knows the thoughts of a man except the man's spirit within him? In the same way no one knows the thoughts of God except the Spirit of God."

When a person receives Christ as their personal savior, the Holy Spirit comes to make His home in them, and the Holy Spirit knows the mind of God.

> John 16:15 (Jesus) "All that belongs to the Father is mine. That is why I said the Spirit will take from what is mine and make it known to you."

Since the Spirit lives in us and since He knows the mind of God, one of His jobs is to reveal God's wisdom to us. He reveals the things of God to us. He imparts wisdom and reveals truth to our spirit and our spirit teaches or enlightens *"the eyes of our heart"* or our mind.

As a sincere Christ follower, you are spiritual, and you are natural. Wouldn't you agree that the natural doesn't always understand the spiritual. So, it is important that our minds be enlightened or tutored by the Spirit to know what's going on in our spirit.

The Holy Spirit wants us to know what it is to be enlightened but the mind often misses what the Spirit is saying or attempting to reveal because it's too busy. A mind that is too busy is abnormal. The mind is normal when it is at rest – not blank, but at rest.

Our minds should not be filled with fear, worry, anxiety and a variety of rationalizations. They should be calm, even serene.

We need to keep our minds in "normal mode," if you will. If they are in some other condition, that would explain why we have very little revealed to us by the Holy Spirit, and why we often feel that we lack wisdom and divine revelation.

Lights On

The Holy Spirit wants to turn the lights on in your mind by giving information from God to your spirit, and your spirit and mind are to help one another. But if your mind is too busy it will miss what the Lord is attempting to reveal to you.

The Lord spoke to Elijah after he had the major showdown with the 450 prophets of Baal, who were all killed. He had just seen God do this miraculous thing with the sacrifices being consumed by fire from heaven. King Ahab's wife, Jezebel, is outraged and swears that she is going to have Elijah killed. So, Elijah runs away and hides.

Now he's depressed and he even prayed that he might die. (1 Kings 19:4) Wow, talk about mood swings. This man of God goes from a victory and an emotional high to an emotional low and wanting to die.

I've been in ministry for nearly five decades and I can relate to Elijah. I have experienced similar emotions. After an amazing Holy Spirit filled ministry Sunday when the adrenaline is pumping, I felt highly energized.

Then comes Monday morning. That is when I have experienced the emotional low. After a spiritual high there is often an emotional low. Now that I've come to expect it, that dramatic low is almost completely gone or at least very short-lived.

God Speaks

> 1 Kings 19:11-12 "The Lord said to Elijah, 'Go out and stand on the mountain in the presence of the Lord, for the Lord is about to pass by.' Then a great and powerful wind tore the mountains apart and shattered the rocks before the Lord, but the Lord was not in the wind. After the wind there was an earthquake, but the Lord was not in the earthquake. [12] After the earthquake came a fire, but the Lord was not in the fire. And after the fire came a gentle whisper."

Some translations say, "a still small voice." Did you know we can ask for God to reveal things to us? He reveals things to us by His Spirit.

If you are not receiving much from God, maybe it is because you're not asking. Or maybe it is because your mind is so wild and busy that you miss the information.

Let's say two people are talking at a big 30-year anniversary celebration. The band is playing, the caterer is cleaning up the dishes, people are talking, and your friend is trying to whisper a secret in your ear. You miss most of what they are saying because the room is so noisy. Unless you're paying very close attention you may not even know that they are speaking to you.

Gentle Holy Spirit

The way of the Holy Spirit is gentle. Most of the time the way He speaks to us is in a still small voice. A prompting in your spirit or a new thought into your mind. If there is a lot of noise and distractions in your mind you will miss it.

> Isaiah 26:3 "You will keep in perfect peace him whose mind is steadfast, because he trusts in you."

Your mind and your spirit work together. The devil will, of course, try to overload and overwork your mind, filling it with all kinds of wrong thoughts. This is so you won't be free and available to the Holy Spirit and Him speaking to your spirit.

Our minds should be kept peaceful. Isaiah said that when a mind is stayed on the right things it will be at rest.

Not Sleepy – When I say at rest don't hear sleepy! We are to be alert.

Three Abnormal Conditions of Our Mind

1. <u>Wandering Mind (Wondering Mind)</u>

Your mind can be wandering all over the place. There is an inability to concentrate. This is often an attack from the enemy. Let me explain. Many people have for years let their minds wander all over the place and they have never disciplined them.

If this is you, you may have thought you were mentally lacking. The inability to concentrate may be the result of years of letting your mind do whatever it wants to do, whenever it wants to do it. Besides a spiritual attack, the lack of concentration could be the result of a poor diet or extreme fatigue. These things can affect your ability to concentrate well.

I've found that when I'm really tired the devil attacks my mind. He knows it is difficult to resist him when I'm mentally exhausted. He wants us to passively accept whatever lies he tells us.

Wander means to roam about aimlessly. Has this happened to you? You're sitting in church on Sunday and you're enjoying the message, you're benefiting from what is being said, and then suddenly your mind begins to wander. In your mind you are somewhere else. Finally, you wake up and you can't remember a thing. Your body was there but not your mind. My friend says, *"You were in La La land."*

Remember that in spiritual warfare your mind is the battlefield. That's where the enemy makes his attack. You might think that since the devil went to the trouble to attack with a wandering mind then maybe there is something being said that you need to hear. Discipline your mind by listening to the sermon again until you get it.

2. <u>A Confused Mind</u>

A confused mind is cousin to a wandering mind.

> James 1:5-8 "If any of you lacks wisdom, he should ask God, who gives generously to all without finding fault, and it will be given to him. [6] But when he asks, he must believe and not doubt, because he who doubts is like a wave of the sea, blown and tossed by the wind. [7]That man should not think he will receive anything from the Lord; [8] he is a double-minded man, unstable in all he does."

A double-minded person is a person of two minds. They are a picture of confusion. Constantly going back and forth, never deciding on anything. As soon as they decide, here comes doubt holding hands with wondering and confusion.

Matthew 16:8 When Jesus is talking to the disciples he said, "Why are you talking among yourselves?" (KJV "Why are you reasoning among yourselves?")

Reasoning basically means trying to figure out the why behind something. Reasoning causes the mind to revolve around and around a situation or issue or event, attempting to understand all of it. We are reasoning when we dissect a statement or teaching to see if it is logical, and we disregard it if it's not.

The devil frequently steals the will of God from us due to reasoning. The Lord may tell you to do a certain thing, but it doesn't make sense, it is not logical, and so we may be tempted to disregard it.

Have you discovered that God doesn't always ask you to do what is "logical"? Your spirit may affirm it, but your mind rejects it, especially if it is difficult or unpleasant or requires personal sacrifice.

Don't reason in your mind when God tells you to do something, just obey Him.

The Spirit of God has often told me to call a certain person on the phone. Or give some money to a certain person/family. I was obedient and did it. It turned out to be just what that person needed at that moment.

One time the Lord told me to drive over to the church. It was a cold and rainy day, so I was a bit reluctant. After about the third time, I felt this strong impression to drive to the church and I finally went. My wife was there but she was in a counseling appointment. I went outside and started to pull a few weeds when a car pulled in the parking lot. I kind of recognized the driver. I thought I had seen him in church, maybe once. He got out and said that he wanted to make a donation to the church. He then handed me a check for $10,00.00! He then got back in his car and drove off - I never saw him again.

Just do it. Listen to the Lord and do what He says.

The Natural Man

The natural man doesn't understand the spiritual man. The natural or carnal man can't reconcile giving away money when he needs money. He can't reason in his mind to give a car away or to go to a certain place on a cold rainy day. To the natural mind it doesn't make sense!

> 1 Corinthians 2:14 "The man without the Spirit does not accept the things that come from the Spirit of God, for they are foolishness to him, and he cannot understand them, because they are spiritually discerned."

> James 1:22 "Do not merely listen to the word, and so deceive yourselves. Do what it says."

Any time that we hear what the word of God is saying and refuse to do it, reasoning has gotten into our thinking to deceive us.

I've found that God wants me to obey Him whether I feel like it or not, or think it's a good idea or not. I have learned to do it immediately.

When God speaks through His word or in our spirit, we are not to reason or debate – just to do it.

3.   <u>The Worried and Anxious Mind</u>

Anxiety and worry are both attacks on the mind that are intended to distract us from serving the Lord. The devil uses both to press down our faith, so that we don't live in victory. Victory is an overcoming life.

> 1 John 5:3-5 "In fact, this is love for God: to keep his commands. And his commands are not burdensome, 4 for everyone born of God overcomes the world. This is the victory that has overcome the world, even our faith. 5 Who is it that overcomes the world? Only the one who believes that Jesus is the Son of God."

Some people may even have such a problem with fear and worry that they are addicted to worrying. If they don't have something of their own to worry about, they'll worry about your stuff!

Jesus came that we might have peace! It is impossible to worry and live in peace at the same time. Peace is not something that can be put on a person. It is a fruit of the Spirit that is referred to in Galatians 5: 22. And the fruit of the Spirit in our lives is a result of abiding in the vine (Jesus) that is referred to in John 15.

Worry, Anxious, Fretting

> 1 Peter 5:7 "Cast all your anxiety/worry/fretting on Him because He cares for you."

Worry is tormenting, isn't it? We torment ourselves with disturbing thoughts. Let me just say it's not smart to torment yourself – you're smarter than that.

You know this – Worry never makes anything better! So why don't we give it up?

Worry can be an attack by the enemy of your soul on your mind. There are certain things that we are instructed to do with our mind and the enemy wants to make sure they are never done.

So, he tries to keep our mental state busy with all kinds of worry, so our mind is not used for the purpose that God intended.

What do you worry about?

Matthew 6:25 tells us that there is nothing in life that we are to worry about.

> "Therefore, I tell you, do not worry about your life, what you will eat or drink; or about your body, what you will wear. Is not life more important than food, and the body more important than clothes?

LIFE is greater than things!

Worry or Concern

Here is the thing about worry. Worry is about the future. We should be concerned about important things but not consumed by worry.

Here is what Jesus said:

> Matthew 6:34 "Therefore do not worry about tomorrow, for tomorrow will worry about itself. Each day has enough trouble of its own."

Worry is spending today trying to figure out tomorrow. Jesus said the devil comes to steal your life with worry!

Don't allow him to do it any longer. Don't spend today worrying about tomorrow. You have enough to do today.

Worry is about the future. However, your task is to stay present. Keep your mind on todays' responsibilities. When you feel yourself getting anxious, fearful, and full of worry, think about what you're thinking about.

Whatever it is, it is out there in the future. It could be three days, three weeks, three years from now!

Bring your thoughts back to today and deal with today. Enjoy today, be present today.

Learn

Learn to cast your cares on the Lord. Learn to cast down arguments and every pretention that sets itself up against the knowledge of God. Cast them down by choosing to think on what is pure, right and true. With the authority of Jesus, rebuke those thoughts and put on what is true.

You will not enter the rest that God has for you without opposition. There is no such thing as peace without opposition. His rest operates in the middle of the storm not in the absence of the storm. The peace that God gives is spiritual and for your inner man.

Jesus didn't come to remove all of the opposition in our lives. If you're waiting to have nothing to worry about before you stop worrying, you're going to have a very long wait.

Being at peace in the middle of the storm and enjoying the rest of God right in the middle of everything going crazy gives glory to the Lord because it proves that His ways work.

You can trust God. That's your part. Don't try to do God's part because you will break under the load.

>Psalm 37:3 "Trust in the Lord and do good; dwell in the land and enjoy safe pasture."

Chapter Seven

Overcoming Depression

We've been talking about how to free your mind. Your mind must be transformed if you hope to mature into the man or woman of God you desire to be. How we think must be transformed. Fair warning: It is a slow process.

Here is a key to transformation: We must have our mind in gear, so to speak, verses a passive mind. What I mean is that we are to discipline our minds and take every thought captive and make it obedient to Christ (2 Corinthians 10:5).

A passive person may want to do the right thing, but they never will unless they purposefully activate their mind to line up with God's word and will. We are often disgusted with ourselves and convicted by the Holy Spirit because of the thoughts we have. Those thoughts may eventually come out of our mouth and in the things that we do.

Before we look at our actions we must back up and look at our thoughts. If we have *stinking thinking* – then what comes out of our mouth and what we do is going to be stinky!

You will not change your behavior until you change your thoughts. What I am saying is right behavior is the fruit of right thinking. We bear the right kind of fruit by abiding in the vine. The vine is Jesus. We're the branches.

> "Remain in me, and I will remain in you. No branch can bear fruit by itself; it must remain in the vine. Neither can you bear fruit unless you remain in me." John 15:4

Abiding in the vine comes down to being obedient to God and His word.

> John 15:10 "If you obey my commands, you will remain in my love, just as I have obeyed my father's commands and remain in his love."

Depression

Feeling depressed is not a new phenomenon. Question: Were there any people in the Bible who wrestled with depression? Yes - King David, Elisha, Jeremiah, and Cain. The Apostle Paul suffered what I will call "the blues."

Let me explain. There is a difference between the blues and depression. Here is what Paul said:

> 2 Corinthians 4:7-9 "But we have this treasure in jars of clay to show that this all-surpassing power is from God

and not from us. ⁸ We are hard pressed on every side, but not crushed; perplexed, but not in despair; ⁹ persecuted, but not abandoned; struck down, but not destroyed."

When I was pastoring in Los Angeles, California, it seemed like I would get depressed every Monday. As you know, Monday is right after Sunday. If Sunday morning church didn't go the way I wanted it to, I would get depressed on Monday. I would slide in a dark pit of despair. I would think, "This isn't working. I am going to fail. My church isn't going to grow." Then I would work all week to climb out of that black hole in time for another Sunday and another Monday. It wasn't until I changed my thinking that the endless cycle of Monday blues went away. I had to agree with Jesus that it was His church. I can't do His part. He said that He would build His church and the gates of hell would not stop Him (Matthew 16:18). And so, I just had to do my part and leave the rest up to Jesus.

In the last few years of my father's life, my siblings and I noticed that my dad had probably been suffering from a long-term low-grade type if depression. My dad was a full-on Christ follower and yet he was tormented by the dark thoughts connected with depression. So many men and women are dealing with depression and not living in the victory that God promises.

What Not to Do

Telling people that they shouldn't feel a certain way is not helpful and it can come off in a condemning way.

What I mean by depression is a very low feeling, a funk, submerged anger, sadness, a feeling that says, "I don't feel like getting out of bed. No, scratch that – I *can't* get out of bed." There is no motivation to do anything. A depressed person might say that they are emotionally drained most of the time. They say, "I may have a few good moments but they never last." The slightest irritation sets off another round of despair.

They may think, "One more bad report and I'll be ready to cash it in.
I can't take it anymore. I don't have the strength to fight. I want to curl up in a ball and die."

That sounds like the Old Testament prophet Elisha after his dramatic showdown with the prophets of Baal on Mount Carmel. When Queen Jezebel heard that Elisha and company had killed the prophets of Baal, she swore that she would kill him. So, Elisha ran away, out into the wilderness, totally depressed and wanted to die.
1 Kings 18:20–40

Everyone feels blue or bummed out at one time or another. Mostly for short periods of time. When these feelings interfere with everyday life then it is kind of like it has taken on a life of its own and we need to do something about it.

It is widely claimed in the medical community that they really don't know the exact cause of depression.

- It could be chemicals in the brain that are out of balance, or
- Stressful events, or
- Part of a person's genetic load

Causes of Depression

Determining the causes of and cures for depression presents a challenge because the symptoms reveal that the whole person, body, soul and spirit is affected.

In the Church, we don't really know how to respond to someone who is struggling emotionally. If someone breaks a leg we flock around, pray for them, and sign their cast.
We can bring meals to their home. We understand physical illness and so we sympathize.
With depression there is "no cast to sign." We don't normally put it out there as a prayer request at church the next Sunday.

Questions: Is there a physical cause to depression, an organic cause? If so, then could there be a physical cure?

Perhaps – but changing brain chemistry is far less certain and precise than changing what we believe or how we think. It has been my experience that it is usually easier to get a person to take a pill with the hope of changing their brain chemistry than it is to get that person to change what they believe or how they think.

Jesus

I want to start by saying that Jesus can relate to our weakness. The book of Hebrews teaches that Jesus came in the flesh and was tempted and tried as a man (Hebrews 4:14–15).

Jesus went through a lot. He voluntarily surrendered his divine attributes. During his life, all of the political and religious forces were against him. In the end he was alone. Even his chosen disciple deserted him. Peter denied him, and even that he ever knew him. Jesus was grieved to the point of death in the Garden of Gethsemane. He was well acquainted with sorrow and grief.

Finally, He faced a mockery of a trial and was found guilty. Jesus, the most innocent man who ever lived was brutally crucified.

Hebrews 4 tells us that we can go to God in our time of need because of Jesus.

> Hebrews 4:14–16 14"Therefore, since we have a great high priest who has gone through the heavens, Jesus the Son of God, let us hold firmly to the faith we profess. [15] For we do not have

a high priest who is unable to sympathize with our weaknesses, but we have one who has been tempted in every way, just as we are—yet was without sin. [16] Let us then approach the throne of grace with confidence, so that we may receive mercy and find grace to help us in our time of need."

Jesus made it possible for us to go to God, not only because he died for our sin, <u>but</u> also because He, by his own experience, can relate to our weakness. Moreover, He has the power to help us. We have the assurance that if we go to God, we will receive mercy and find grace to help us in our time of need.

Do You Need Help?

Today, I want to help establish your hope in God and enable you to live according to the truth of God's word.

Perhaps you are struggling right now. There's a fight on the inside. Some internal hostilities. Maybe you feel like you're slipping, or that you are really messed up. May I say to you - respond to the Holy Spirit's promptings. Admit where you are and what you are feeling to the Lord. Ask for and receive God's mercy. His mercies are new every morning. Receive God's grace in Jesus' name! And then hold steady.

I have a saying that helps me: "Talk to yourself and don't let yourself talk to you."

What do I mean by that? You are a spirit, you have a soul, and you live in a body. The struggle is between your soul and your spirit. Your soul is where your feelings and emotions live, and your spirit is the part of you that communes with God. Your spirit knows the right thing to do but your soul does not feel like doing it. Your spirit must dictate to your soul what you will do.

Do not try to fix your feelings. Rather, do the next right thing and fulfill the next responsibility that you have, and your feelings will catch up.

Hope

Let me say to you that truth restores hope. Research reveals that there is a link between brain chemistry and hope, meaning that your body is affected by what you think.

If we think we are helpless, hopeless and out of control then these thoughts may lead to symptoms of depression. These include sadness, despair, lethargy, loss of appetite and sleep problems. However, once hope is restored, depression leaves. We are no longer in a "low" place, we become "level" or "on par," so to speak.

Faith

God established faith as the way that you relate to Him, and the way that you are to live your life. As a Christ follower, you live by faith. However, God doesn't bypass our minds.

I'll ask this question again, "Does what you think about affect how you feel?" The answer is yes. So, how do we change our thoughts and beliefs?

Follow this - we know that physical pain is necessary for our survival. Like a flame will burn you so that you do not touch it. If we see a sign like "Danger High Voltage," we know not to touch it. If we are at the beach and there is a sign, "Caution - Sharks**,"** we do not go in the water.

In a similar way, when we're in emotional pain it stimulates the process for us to renew our mind by faith. It is part of developing our character.

Did you know that you are never commanded in scripture to change your feelings? You are, however, commanded to change your deeds. This is inclusive of your thoughts, your words and your actions!

You may ask, how do I do that?

Think and Believe

How does our thinking affect our emotions? Even though we have very little control over our emotions, we can change how we think and what we believe.

Secular cognitive therapists like Albert Ellis and Aaron Beck teach that our emotions are essentially a product of our thoughts. They believe that the primary source of depression is the way that people perceive themselves, their circumstances and their futures, which are referred to as the "depression triad."

Follow this: Cognitive (mental) therapy is based on the premise that people do what they do and feel what they feel because of what they choose to think and believe. As a result, if we want to change how we behave or feel, what should we do? We should change what we think and believe.

From a Christian perspective, that is repentance. If we possess distorted, false or negative beliefs about God, ourselves and the world, then we disagree with what God says about Himself, us and the world in which we live. This "disagreement" is missing the mark, and it is sin.

> Romans 14:23 "Whatever is not of faith is sin."

Confession and Repentance

Confession is agreeing with God. When God the Holy Spirit convicts you of something you must agree or say the same thing about it that He is saying. If He says it's sin, then call it sin. Here's why. There is a remedy for sin.

> 1 John 1:9 "If we confess our sin, He is faithful and just to forgive us and cleans us from all unrighteousness."

Repentance is always connected to confession. Repentance happens when old worldly beliefs are replaced with biblical godly beliefs. That is, beliefs that are based on God's word.

Repentance is a change of mind. It must happen if we are going to have a liberated life in Christ. It is a daily choice.

Last week I woke up at 4:30 am and by 5:00 am my mind was going, and the fight was on to keep my thoughts focused on what was true. It was a fight that took three or four hours. I began to quote scriptures aloud and speak in faith. I began to proclaim the truth. I was fighting to keep my mind in a righteous place. You speak the truth, and it sets you free.

I began to speak in faith and to speak righteously and positively. It was not based on how I was feeling. I was speaking in faith and choosing to believe the truth of God's word. After a few hours, my feelings caught up with my faith.

If you have little knowledge about God and His word, you will have little faith. Speak this in faith, "I can do all things through Christ who strengthens me."

Say it again.

Struggling

Here is what I've noticed: Depressed people are negative people. I heard one pastor describe it this way, "You have ANT brain – Automatic Negative Thoughts." They think negative or unrighteous thoughts. They say negative things to you and me, and that reinforces the negative thinking. They do not speak in faith. They are not speaking life, rather they speak death.

> Proverbs 18:21 "The tongue has the power of life and death, and those who love it will eat its fruit."

In my struggle I recalled a passage in Lamentations 3:19-26:

> 19 I remember my affliction and my wandering, the bitterness and the gall. 20 I well remember them, and my soul is downcast within me. 21 Yet this I call to mind and therefore I have hope: 22 Because of the LORD's great love we are not consumed, for his compassions never fail. 23 They are new every morning; great is your faithfulness. 24 **I say to myself,** "The LORD is my portion; therefore, I will wait for him." 25 The LORD is good to those whose hope is in him, to the one who seeks him; 26 it is good to wait quietly for the salvation of the LORD.

The author of Lamentations, Jeremiah, took charge of his thoughts. He was talking to *himself* and not letting *himself* talk to him. He remembered all of the true things about the Lord.

Back to my 4:30 wake up. As I laid there on my bed that morning, I took charge of my thoughts. I disciplined my mind. It was a fight. I had to fight to look up to the Lord because I was starting to lose my focus.

Focus

What should be our focus? Jesus gave us the answer in Matthew 22:36–40:

> "Love the Lord your God with all your heart with all your soul with all your mind. This is the first and greatest commandment. And the second is like it; love your neighbor as yourself. All the law and the prophets hang on these two commandments."

When you're heading into a low state of mind what are you thinking about? Where is your focus? Your focus is on yourself.

When you are feeling depressed where is your focus? It is not on God and others. You must fight to get your focus back and believe God and his word.

Use your Weapons: The word, prayer, and praise and worship.

Red Flag Warning

God has designed a feedback system to grab your attention so that you can examine your goals and beliefs. When an experience or relationship leaves you feeling angry, anxious or depressed, those are emotional signposts that are alerting you that you may be cherishing a faulty goal based on a wrong belief.

For example, let's look at anger. When you are in a relationship or doing some project with someone else and it results in feelings of anger, it usually means that someone, or something, has blocked your goal. You were prevented from accomplishing what you wanted to do. You had an expectation that went unmet.

Think about finding yourself in a traffic jam that is going to make you late for your next appointment. Your goal was to arrive on time, and that goal has been blocked.

As another example, a Christian wife and mother who says, "My goal is to have a loving, harmonious, and happy Christian family." Question: "Who can block her goal?" Answer: "Every person in her family." Not only can they, but they will.

Follow this - every time that her husband or children fail to live up to her image as a "happy family," on which she has staked her self-worth, while thinking, "I'm a good mother and wife because we are all happy."

– her feeling of self-worth will crash and burn each time. She could then become very angry and controlling, and start driving her family members away from her as a result.

Depression

Depression signals an impossible goal. When you base your future success on something that can never happen you have an impossible goal. Your depression is a signal that your goal, no matter how good, lofty, spiritual or altruistic, may never be reached.

We can be depressed for biochemical reasons as well. This is why it is important to inform your doctor if you are depressed and to get a complete checkup. Then if there is no physical cause, your depression will often be rooted in a sense of hopelessness and/or helplessness. Again, if you have been feeling depressed for some time, you should go to your doctor and get a complete physical.

Goals and Desires

To live successful lives, we need to distinguish a godly goal from an ungodly desire. This is liberating and it gives inner peace.

A godly goal reflects God's purpose in your life and is not dependent on other people or circumstances beyond your ability or right to control. The only person who can block a godly goal or render it uncertain is you. If you adopt an attitude of cooperation with the

Holy Spirit and His goals for your life, just as Jesus' mother Mary did, your goal can be reached.

An ungodly desire is any specific result that depends on the cooperation of other people whom you have no right or ability to control. You cannot base your success or self-worth on your incorrect desires, no matter how godly they are, because you cannot control their fulfillment. We know that some of our desires will be blocked and eventually prove impossible. Because life doesn't always go our way.

We will struggle with anger, anxiety and depression when we elevate a *desire* to a *goal* in our minds. By comparison, when a desire isn't met you will only face disappointment.
We all have disappointments in life. Dealing with disappointment is easier than dealing with anger, anxiety and depression.

Does God Have any Desires or Goals?

Yes!
> Ezekiel 18:31 "For I have no pleasure in the death of anyone who dies, declares the Lord. Therefore, repent and live."

It's God's desire that we would all repent and live, but you know not all will. John the beloved wrote,

> "My little children, I am writing these things to you that you might not sin."
> 1 John 2:1

Think about this: God's success or integrity is not dependent upon whether or not we sin. God has no blocked goals. It is His desire that everyone repent, but some will not.

When you begin to align your goals with God's goals and your desires with God's desires, you will rid your life of a lot of anger, anxiety and depression.

Remember the mother who wants a harmonious home. It is a ungodly desire that she cannot guarantee. Her goal, rather, would be to become the wife and mother that God wants her to be. The only one who can block that goal for her is herself.

Self-Centered

Symptoms of depression are often precipitated by some self-centered sin. In such cases, we are living to please ourselves rather the Lord. If you don't turn away from it, and by that I mean repent and agree with what the Holy Spirit is convicting you of, and if you do not confess your self-centeredness and return to living for the Lord, then you will experience even further challenges.

May I encourage you to turn from going your way and to go God's way. "You'll love life and see good days." 1 Peter 3:10

Feelings

Don't try to fix your feelings. They will come along in due time. You just do the next right thing before God and your feelings will catch up.

No matter how difficult any situation appears, Jesus said "*I have overcome it.*"

> John 16:33 "I have told you these things, so that in me you may have peace. In this world you will have trouble. But take heart! I have overcome the world."

God will not allow anything into your life that is beyond His control or beyond your ability to deal with it without sinning (1 Corinthians 10:13).

God is the God of all comfort. His mercies are new every morning!

Chapter Eight

Overcome

What does overcome mean? It means to prevail over, to conquer as in a struggle; to conquer something, to get the better of something. We want to overcome depression!

We've been talking about changing the way that we think, and that it is a battle. I think you would agree with that. We know that the transformation of our mind is a progressive, inch-by-inch choice that we make daily.

The *Great Theologian* Dr. Seuss said, "You have brains in your head, you have feet in your shoes, you can steer yourself any direction you choose."

Outside of the Holy Spirit, your power to choose is the most powerful ability you have in your battle to transform your mind. It is impossible to get from wrong behavior to right behavior without first changing your thoughts. So, we're in a battle in our mind.

Fight

If we are in a battle, then we must fight!

We talked about the three weapons that we must use to fight the battle that goes on in our minds. The Word of God, Prayer and

Praise. A fourth weapon is to talk to a growing Christian friend. You could say a confidante. I would like to emphasize the word *growing*. They are increasing in their relationship with God and His word - increasing spiritually.

I've said this several times but let me say it again: "You will not change your behavior until you change your thoughts. You now know that we are never commanded in scripture to change your feelings. We are, however, commanded to change our deeds. Remember that deeds are inclusive of our thoughts, our words and our actions.

Blocked Goals

We talked about blocked goals and desires, and how these play into depression. When you begin to align your goals with God's goals and your desires with Gods desires you will rid your life of a lot of anger, anxiety and depression.

Jesus gave us our focus in life. This bears repeating - I call it "The Big L." Again, it comes from Matthew 22:37–40.

> 37 Jesus replied: "'Love the Lord your God with all your heart and with all your soul and with all your mind. 38 This is the first and greatest commandment. 39 And the second is like it: 'Love your neighbor as yourself.' 40 All the Law and the

> Prophets hang on these two commandments."

We tend to complicate things, but Jesus simplified the Jewish law into two simple commands. Here it is, Love God with all your heart, soul and mind; Love your neighbor as yourself. "The Big L."

This must be our motivation in all that we do. Why? because we love the Lord. We're motivated by love, meaning that we want the highest good for the other person. It doesn't mean that you have to be best friends and go on vacation together with whomever, but you sincerely want God's best for them.

Depression

What is the emotion of depression like? Depression is that low feeling, like you're living in a dark hole. You are not motivated to do anything. It's been said that, "Depression is an ache in the soul that crushes the spirit." A constant feeling of sadness with difficulty concentrating.

Depression is a natural consequence when we experience losses in our lives. And so we need to know how to respond to loss. Losing a job, a loved one, or our health are all tough. However, it is God's intention to grow us through these tough times. It is a time to learn how to overcome feelings of helplessness and hopelessness. Hal Lindsay said, "We can live forty days without food, about three days without water, and about eight minutes without air, but only one second without hope!" It has been said that the richest treasures are often found in the deepest holes.

Restoring Hope

What we will teach today will restore your hope. Here is the axiom - Truth Restores Hope!

As you know, depression is an epidemic in our world, touching millions of people around the globe. Twice as many women as men struggle with depression. Even college students struggle with depression. It seems those who are able to set their own schedules are particularly susceptible to feelings of depression. These are people like homemakers, salesmen, pastors and college students. It is as common as the common cold.

Research done in America has shown that over half of us will struggle with depression at least once in our lifetimes and that everyone will experience some depression symptoms. They are due to such factors as poor health, some negative circumstance(s) or a weak spiritual condition. It is this Spiritual part that where I am trying to help you.

Listen to this description of depression: "It is a disturbance or disorder in one's mood or emotional state."

- It is characterized by persistent sadness, heaviness, darkness or feelings of emptiness.
- The emotional state of depression is usually accompanied by thoughts of hopelessness and sometimes suicide.
- Depressed people believe life is bad and any hope for improvement is non-existent.
- Their thoughts are colored by negative and pessimistic views of themselves, their future and their circumstances.

The Cause

Most professionals in the medical field will admit that the causes of depression are largely unknown. It is important to understand that the emotional state of depression is not a cause, it is symptomatic of something deeper. Treating this symptom only brings temporary relief at best. We need to focus on the root cause(s) and not the symptom(s). They can be physical, mental and/or spiritual.

Physical

When was the last time you went to the doctor and had a complete physical? If there are some identifiable symptoms, then get checked out by your doctor.

Be cautious about the meds. A CBS investigative television show called "60 Minutes" did a story on depression on

February 29, 2012. The doctors interviewed said that people with mild depression were part of a clinical trial. Half the people took the real antidepressant drug, and the other half of the group took the placebo. What do you think the outcome was? The outcome was virtually the same.

I'd recommend working on your thought life and your beliefs first before taking antidepressant medications.

Indicators

This is what we know, emotions are indicators. They are like the lights on the dashboard in your car. Depression is signaling that something happened - probably a loss of some kind. For most people there is a thought process that needs adjusting or complete reprogramming. If it is a chronic problem, just like with a car, you must look under the hood, so to speak.

That acknowledgement of *looking under the hood* is called being honest about your feelings so that you can resolve their cause and live in harmony with God and other people.

If you've read the Bible much then you know that the term depression isn't there. However, many of the symptoms associated with depression are there. The scripture describes the emotional upset that a person feels.

The Bible says things like this that describe depression:

- Having a fallen countenance, Genesis 4:7
- Having a broken spirit, Proverbs 17:22
- Being sad, Proverbs 15:13
- Experiencing despair, Psalms 42:11
- Being broken hearted, Psalms 147:3
- Being burdened by the weight of sin, Psalms 38:4
- Mourning, Psalms 38:6
- Greatly bowed down, having grief, losing heart/faint/ weary, etc.

Depression has both deeds and feelings associated with it. Remember that those deeds include your thoughts, words, and actions. Most people think that getting rid of depression is equivalent to getting rid of certain unwanted feelings. We are learning that it is more than that.

Feelings

We are not responsible for how we feel. Feelings just are. They are indicators. We are responsible for what we **do** with those feelings. This is very important as we look at overcoming depression. This is also exciting because there is tremendous hope for a person who is depressed.

God doesn't judge us based on our feelings. He judges us based on our obedience. It is wonderful and reassuring to know that even if we are feeling miserable God is pleased if we do what He instructs us to do.

Example: Elijah

> 1 Kings 19:1-5 "Now Ahab told Jezebel everything Elijah had done and how he had killed all the prophets with the sword. ² So Jezebel sent a messenger to Elijah to say, "May the gods deal with me, be it ever so severely, if by this time tomorrow I do not make your life like that of one of them."³ Elijah was afraid and ran for his life. When he came to Beersheba in Judah, he left his servant there, ⁴ while he himself went a day's journey into the desert. He came to a broom tree, sat down under it and prayed that he might die. "I have had enough, Lord," he said. "Take my life; I am no better than my ancestors." ⁵ Then he lay down under the tree and fell asleep."

What was he feeling? Afraid. So, he ran for his life, and gave into despair so much that he just wanted to die. Why? To end all of the bad feelings. Remember that this happened after seeing God do a miraculous thing with the prophets of Baal.

Example: Jonah

> Jonah 4:1-11 "But Jonah was greatly displeased and became angry. ² He prayed to the Lord, "O Lord, is this not

what I said when I was still at home? That is why I was so quick to flee to Tarshish. I knew that you are a gracious and compassionate God, slow to anger and abounding in love, a God who relents from sending calamity. ³ Now, O LORD, take away my life, for it is better for me to die than to live." ⁴ But the LORD replied, "Have you any right to be angry?"
⁵ Jonah went out and sat down at a place east of the city. There he made himself a shelter, sat in its shade and waited to see what would happen to the city. ⁶ Then the LORD God provided a vine and made it grow up over Jonah to give shade for his head to ease his discomfort, and Jonah was very happy about the vine. ⁷ But at dawn the next day God provided a worm, which chewed the vine so that it withered. ⁸ When the sun rose, God provided a scorching east wind, and the sun blazed on Jonah's head so that he grew faint. He wanted to die, and said, "It would be better for me to die than to live." ⁹ But God said to Jonah, "Do you have a right to be angry about the vine?" "I do," he said. "I am angry enough to die."
¹⁰ But the LORD said, "You have been concerned about this vine, though you did not tend it or make it grow. It sprang up overnight and died overnight. ¹¹ But Nineveh has more than a hundred and twenty thousand people who cannot tell their right hand

from their left, and many cattle as well. Should I not be concerned about that great city?"

What was he feeling? Angry, frustrated, and he didn't like what God was doing. He was angry with God, and he wanted to die. Again, get me out of these bad feelings!

Maybe you can identify with Jonah. You don't like what God is doing. In you there is a submerged anger. You had an expectation that God would do something a certain way and He didn't do it that way. Here is the progression – an unmet expectation turns into hurt feelings and then anger. Often then that anger comes out on those closest to us.

Not Responsible

We are not responsible for our feelings, but we are responsible for our deeds (thoughts, words and actions). There is a difference between the feelings associated with depression and the sinful deeds associated with depression.

Feelings of depression are sometimes precipitated by some rebellion or sin. Do you know what that means? That means that you're living to please yourself instead of living to please the Lord. If you don't turn away, that is repent and truly confess your self-centeredness, and begin to live in a way that honors the Lord your problems will only get worse.

How do I change?

Remember the "Big L" – Love God, Love others. The change in your life started when you said yes to Jesus and began to follow Him. Let me say it another way, change begins at spiritual birth and continues throughout your life.

Your purpose in living changes from a focus of living for yourself to one of dying to yourself as you learn to love God and love others in a way that lines up with the what the Bible teaches us.

Wouldn't you agree that God's ways are better than your ways? By better I mean superior.

> Isaiah 55:9 "As the heavens are higher than the earth, so are my ways higher than your ways and my thoughts than your thoughts."

You would also agree that His word is truth.

> Psalms 119:160 "All your words are true; all your righteous laws are eternal."

Follow this: If you neglect or refuse God's way or His truth, you will experience ever-increasing problems and the problems you have will get worse.

If you neglect or refuse God's direction in your life and choose to follow the path of least resistance, i.e. your feelings and desires or what seems good at the moment, that is "the quick fix," then you will be headed for your own undoing and ruin.

Three Levels of the Problem

Level One: Heart.
Level Two: Doing.
Level Three: Feelings.

A problem starts in the heart and then often leads us into a downward spiral. Have you heard that saying, "Follow your heart"? Here is what the Bible says about that:

> Jeremiah 17:9-10. "The heart is deceitful above all things and beyond cure; who can understand it?"

The heart problem leads to unbiblical deeds, i.e. unbiblical thoughts, words, and actions. Then these deeds are often accompanied by and lead to bad feelings. You may remember the story of Cain and Abel. In Genesis 4:5 we learn that Cain brought an unacceptable offering to the Lord. When the Lord didn't accept it, he became "very angry and his face was downcast."

But in the next two verses God give the remedy to his problem:

> 6 Then the Lord said to Cain, "Why are you angry? Why is your face downcast? 7 If you do what is right, will you not be accepted? But if you do

not do what is right, sin is crouching at your door; it desires to have you, but you must rule over it."

Downward Spiral

Suppose you are a college student or maybe a salesman looking at all of the homework or a stack of cold call sales contacts. Or perhaps you could be a mom or dad looking at a huge pile of laundry…

Student

A. Heart level: His focus is on himself. Jesus said in Luke 9:23-24 "If you want to come after me you must deny yourself and take up your cross and follow me. (Follow Jesus– follow His example and teaching.) For whoever wants to save his life will lose it and whoever loses his life for my sake will find it."

B. Doing level: Making choices - he starts with a thought. He is tempted to do what he's feeling like: play ball, go to the beach, go see his girlfriend...

- He's lazy – he doesn't want to study – *thoughts* – he comes up with excuses.

- So, he doesn't study – *actions.*

- He goes and hangs out with the guys – goofing off – *actions.*

- He worries about failing the course – *thoughts.*

- He lies to his parents about being ready for the exam – *words.*

- He cheats on the exam – *actions.*

- He fails the course – *consequences.*

C. Feeling level: Now he is feeling depression, despair, and guilt.

What's the world's solution to bad feelings? Often it is to self-medicate with things like using alcohol, overeating, shopping, etc.

The typical "solutions" (or the world's solutions) to your difficulties will ultimately fail because they don't deal with the source of your problem, which is your heart.

God's solutions go to the heart of the matter, where permanent change is accomplished.

How Do You Know Where to Start to Make Changes?

The first thing to do is to commit to God's leadership in your life.

Commit to His sovereignty and surrender to Him.

- Invite Jesus Christ into your life to be your savior and determine to live each

day for Him. That means to live in a way that pleases Him.
- Determine specific ways that you have sinned against God. Since those ways are contrary to scripture and displeasing to God you must turn away from them. That means to repent.
- Ask God for wisdom to know what changes to make and how to make them. Ask in faith and He will answer you.

Back to our College Student – how does he get out of the pit of feeling depressed?

Living God's way means putting away your self-centeredness and committing yourself to following God's word despite any feelings to the contrary.

Building Hope

Building hope into your life starts with confession and repentance. It is to confess to God and be specific about the recognized sins. See Psalms 51:1–10. As you pray, commit your life and your way to the Lord, without reservation. Go all in! Not one foot in the world and one in the Lord. 100% for the Lord while putting yourself aside.

What I mean is to be self-forgetful. That is put yourself on the back burner in your thinking.

Seldom do we ever need encouragement to love ourselves. As a matter of fact, the Bible says that we already do, and that is the problem.

> Ephesians 5:29 "After all, no one ever hated their own body, but they feed and care for their body, just as Christ does the church."

For example, when you are in a group picture, and you look at the picture, who is the first person you see? YOU! And, by the way, if you don't look good in the picture then it is a bad picture. Because it is all about you.

To build hope you must stay tender to the Holy Spirit. What I mean is that when He speaks to you, you do what He says. He will speak to you through His word, the Bible, through an impression, or a prompt in your spirit. You might say a nudge in your spirit. You will know it is Him because it is a good, pleasing and godly idea.

As we read in Philippians 4:6–9, "Keep your mind on what is true, honorable, right, pure, lovely, excellent and praiseworthy." Set your mind on the things above (Colossians 3:2).

The apostle Paul mentions two more things that will help build hope in your life. He says to be others focused and that includes being compassionate and offering forgiveness. This carries with it an opportunity for reconciliation, where you return a blessing for the evil done to you.

Finally, speak the truth in love. And speak in faith as we have mentioned before, by the choice of my will I will rejoice. I say, I can do all things through Christ who strengthens me. Speak to the Lord regularly – pray. God's peace and joy will return.

No matter how difficult your situation appears, Jesus Christ has overcome it. "I have overcome the world." John 16:33

More Hope

The truth is that God will not allow anything into your life that is beyond His control or beyond your ability to endure it without sinning.

> 1 Cor 10:13 "No temptation has seized you except what is common to man. And God is faithful; he will not let you be tempted beyond what you can bear. But when you are tempted, he will also provide a way out so that you can stand up under it."

I need to tell you something: Trials and tests are for your good.

> Romans 5:3-5. "Not only so, but we also rejoice in our sufferings, because we know that suffering produces perseverance; [4] perseverance,

character; and character, hope. [5] And hope does not disappoint us, because God has poured out his love into our hearts by the Holy Spirit, whom he has given us."

KEY – As you respond to tests/temptations/trials in a godly and biblical way you give opportunity for the power of God to show up in your life.

2 Corinthians 12:9-10 "But he [Jesus] said to me, 'My grace is sufficient for you, for my power is made perfect in weakness.' Therefore, I will boast all the more gladly about my weaknesses, so that Christ's power may rest on me. [10] That is why, for Christ's sake, I delight in weaknesses, in insults, in hardships, in persecutions, in difficulties. For when I am weak, then I am strong."

God's comfort and care holds us in our difficulties.

Now what?

We must put off all of the disobedient stuff. That is, disobedience to God's word and the conviction of the Holy Spirit. And then put on a life of faithfulness. Put on a life that yields to God. And when we hear the Word of God speaking to us, we say "YES, YES, YES, I will."

Why? Because we are committed to pleasing Jesus. We love the Lord and want to please Him. We are not doing the right thing for other people or the church, BUT because we love the Lord.

Do

We all have some God given responsibilities. You must take them up regardless of any feelings of depression that you may have. This is the key. Carry out these responsibilities wholeheartedly as unto the Lord. Why? Because you love the Lord.

If you sin then confess it and turn away from it. If you sin against someone, then go to them and make it right, that is to confess and ask for forgiveness.

God has promised to take care of all of your needs as you seek His Kingdom and His righteousness. How do you do this? By keeping your spiritual eyes firmly fixed on Jesus and following in His footsteps daily.

Bibliography

Anderson, Neil, *Bondage Breaker*, Harvest House Publishers, Eugene, Oregon, 1993.

Biblegateway.com, updated June 2023.

Broger, John, *Self-Confrontation,* Biblical Counseling Foundation, Commonwealth of Virginia, 1991.

GotQuestions.com, updated June 2023.

Hayford, Jack, *Hayford's Bible Handbook,* Thomas Nelson Publishers, Nashville, Tennessee, 1995.

Healthline.com, updated 2024.

Hunt, T.W., *The Mind of Christ*, Broadman & Holman Publishers, Nashville, Tennessee, 1995.

Meyer, Joyce, *Battlefield of the Mind,* Harrison House, Tulsa, Oklahoma, 1995.

Mowry, Bill, *The Ways of the Leader,* NavPress, The Navigators, Colorado Springs, Colorado, 2023.

Made in the USA
Columbia, SC
16 June 2024